# bobby hull THE GOLDEN JET

## by Ted Zalewski

## Illustrated By John Nelson

Text copyright © 1974 by Educreative Systems, Inc. Illustrations copyright © 1974 by Creative Education. International copyrights reserved in all countries. No part of this book may be reproduced in any form without written permission from the publisher. Printed in the United States.

Library of Congresss Number: 73-10282     ISBN: O-87191-264-3

Published by Creative Education, Mankato, Minnesota 56001
Prepared for the Publisher by Educreative Systems, Inc.
Distributed by Childrens Press, 1224 West Van Buren Street,Chicago, Illinois 60607

**Library of Congress Cataloging in Publication Data**
Zalewski, Ted.
  Bobby Hull: the Golden Jet.
  1. Hull, Robert Marvin—Juvenile literature.
I. Title. GV848.5.H8Z34 796.9'62'0924 [B] 73-10282 ISBN 0-87191-264-3

"No, he can't do it! I don't believe it," said the skinny man. His foot rested on a car bumper.

"Yes he can," answered Mike. "He's as strong as a tractor. And he's one of the best hockey players around these parts. I know he can do it."

"Then let's get him over here. We'll see if he can do it."

Mike waved his hand at Bob Hull. Bob walked over to the two men who were standing in front of the car.

"My friend doesn't think you can lift up the front end of this car," said Mike. "I told him you're one of the strongest men I know. Can you do it?"

Bob Hull stepped back. He looked from one end of the car to the other. He was a big man, weighing well over 200 pounds. He worked in a cement factory. His arms were large and powerful.

"I'll give it a try."

The skinny man lifted his foot off the bumper. Bob stepped up to the front of the car. He bent down, placing both his hands under the car bumper. He took a deep breath, then lifted. His face turned red. Slowly, the front end of the car rose. The skinny man's eyes popped out. He couldn't believe what he was seeing.

"I told you he could do it," said Mike.

Bob let the car drop to the ground. He rubbed his hands together. His breathing was heavy.

"I'd better go home now. I have to get ready for a game in a few hours."

Bob Hull and his family lived in Pointe Anne, Ontario, Canada. It was a small town of about 100 people. Some people thought that more dogs lived in the town than people. The town had no movies, bars, or shops. It did have two schools and three churches. If you drove out of the town, you would find farm after farm. The city of Toronto was a hundred miles away.

The winters were cold and long in Pointe Anne. Winds swept across the land. Snow covered the ground for many months. All the ponds and lakes were frozen over. They turned into ice skating rinks. So it made sense! The men, women, boys, and girls of Pointe Anne loved to skate. Most of them could skate before they could read.

The Hull family loved to skate too. Poppa Bob Hull especially loved to play hockey. He felt a thrill when he shot the puck at the net. He liked to slam into other players and score goals.

One cold night in Pointe Anne, Mrs. Hull gave birth to her fifth child, a boy named Robert Marvin Hull. The date was January 3, 1939.

Mr. and Mrs. Hull were proud of their new son. They called him Bobby. They didn't know it then, but someday he would be called the "Golden Jet."

As Bobby grew up he liked to watch his father put on his ice skates. The blades gleamed. They were always sharp. The leather smelled good. The shoelaces were as long as Bobby was tall. Poppa Hull pulled his shoelaces tight. He didn't want his skates slipping off. Bobby wished he had a pair of skates.

One Christmas Day, Bobby got his wish. His parents gave him a pair of ice skates. Bobby was only four years old. He put his skates under his arm and took off. Not far from his house was the Bay of Quinte. It was frozen for several months of the year. He wanted to try out his skates right away.

When Bobby got to the lake, he sat down on a log. He pulled off his shoes. Quickly he put on his new skates. He wobbled as he walked to the edge of the lake. He watched the other kids skating across the ice. He knew he could do it.

Bobby stepped out onto the ice. His skates flew up into the air. He tried to grab onto the air with his hands, but it was no use. He landed on his backside on the hard ice.

Bobby sat there a second. He looked at his skates. Nothing was wrong with them. Quickly he got up. He pushed his skates forward. This time he glided along several feet. Then he fell down. He got up. He skated again.

As the day wore on, Bobby learned to skate. He learned to keep his ankles stiff. He learned to use his arms to help him keep his balance. When he wanted to stop, he dug his skates into the ice.

It was late in the afternoon. Bobby was still skating. His cheeks were red and his backside hurt. His legs were sore. When darkness finally came, he didn't think about going home. He skated on and on.

Mrs. Hull became worried about Bobby. She sent her two older daughters to bring him home. They found brother Bobby, skating.

"You have to come home now," shouted one of his sisters.

"Go back home," shouted Bobby. "I want to skate."

The two girls ran out onto the ice. Each of them grabbed one of Bobby's arms. They dragged him home.

"I don't want to go. I want to skate."

Bobby was tired. As soon as he got home, he went to bed. He dreamed of ice skating.

Almost every day, Bobby went to the lake. He would wake up early in the morning. No one was awake. Bobby crept into the kitchen. He made a pot of cooked cereal for himself. Then, as the cereal sat on the stove warming up, he walked to the lake. He skated on the lake. He practiced skating backwards. He took sharp turns. He skated in circles. Then he hurried back home. Waiting for him was a pot of hot cereal!

Bobby grew strong. Besides skating, he shoveled snow. By the time he was eight years old, he had muscles that stood out.

Poppa Hull loved to skate with his son. On a Sunday afternoon they would go to the lake. Bobby would run to get his skates and stick. Together they walked to the lake. After lacing their skates, they eagerly walked to the ice.

Poppa Hull pulled a puck out of his coat pocket. He dropped it onto the ice.

"Now watch."

He pushed the puck out on the ice in front of himself. Then he skated across the ice. The puck led the way. Poppa Hull dug his skates into the ice and stopped. Ice chips flew into the air.

"You take it now."

Bobby put his stick behind the puck. He pushed off on his skates. He glided across the ice. His father skated alongside him.

"Keep your head up. Don't watch the puck."

Bobby lifted up his head.

"Keep your eyes open for defensemen. They'll be charging at you, trying to knock you away from the puck. Be ready to pass. If no one is around you, go for the net," said Poppa Hull.

"From then on," Bobby Hull recalled years later, "I was crazy about the game."

Again and again, Bobby practiced his stick handling. Years later when he played for the Black Hawks, he "would go for the net." Fans would jump up and scream. The Golden Jet would be flying towards the goal. The puck would be out in front of him. A raised stick, a loud smack! The puck would be flying into the net. Another goal!

Almost all Canadian boys play hockey on a team. They begin at five years of age as Peewees. As they grow older and better they can play for the Midgets, Juveniles and Bantams. When they get to be teenagers they can play for the Junior B's and Junior A's. After that they can play hockey on a professional team, if they are good enough. A lot of boys dream of playing for the Red Wings or the Black Hawks someday. Only the best players make it to the "pros."

Bobby Hull played his first Bantam game at the age of 10. He played for the town of Belleville, a village five miles from Pointe Anne. He was such a good player that he passed up playing for the Peewees, the Juveniles and the Midgets. He became a star in the Bantam league.

The Hulls were well known for their hockey playing. One of Bobby's sisters, Judy, was such a rough hockey player that the boys in Pointe Anne said they would not play with her anymore! By the age of 12, Bobby was playing for the same adult team as his father.

Bobby loved hockey so much that he played for more than one team. He played "pond hockey" after school every day. On Saturdays he sometimes played in four different games on four different teams. He would score as many as 25 goals in one day.

Bobby loved to play against other players. His stick-handling, skating and passing improved. He loved to dig the puck out from under the boards. He didn't mind checking hard or getting checked. He was a tough player.

All the professional teams send scouts throughout Canada. They travel from game to game, looking for future stars. They talk with coaches, asking who the best players are. They write down names of players and keep notes on them. It's a hard job. If a player is good, scouts from all the teams might try to sign him up.

Bob Wilson was lucky. In 1953, he was the chief scout of the Chicago Black Hawks. One day Mr. Wilson saw Bobby playing a hockey game. Bobby was 11 years old. Mr. Wilson knew that he was watching a player who would someday be a hockey great.

Mr. Wilson acted quickly. He talked things over with Poppa Hull. "Would you like your son to become a Black Hawk someday?"

Poppa Hull thought about it. His son was so young. Would Bobby be a cement worker like his father? Or could he make a living someday by playing hockey? Would his son be good enough to make it? After much thinking Poppa Hull said "yes."

For the next three years Bobby played hockey. And more hockey. He was waiting for the Black Hawks to send him to a farm team. Finally, when he was 14 years old, the Hawks asked him if he was ready to go. He would have to leave home.

It was a sad time. Hespeler was 170 miles away. Bobby would be leaving his family and home. He would be leaving his friends in Pointe Anne. His chance had come, though! The chance to someday play in the National Hockey League.

When Bobby got to Hespeler, his life changed in many ways. He played on a Junior B team owned by the Hawks. He lived with a different family. He attended a high school where he didn't know anyone.

The Hawks paid him five dollars a week.

His mother wrote him a letter every day, but she didn't say much about Pointe Anne. She was afraid that Bobby would be homesick. Bobby wrote to her, "Gee, Mom, keep all those letters coming with nothing in them."

After Hespeler the Hawks moved Bobby to Galt. He had to attend another high school. It was hard for him. After Galt, he went to Woodstock, then to St. Catherine's. In all, he went to four different high schools. He was suspended from one of them because he didn't follow the rules. However, the school took him back. Bobby never did graduate from high school.

Bobby was 18 years old. He was playing hockey for the St. Catherine's team. He was eating dinner one evening in a boarding house.

"Bobby, there's a long-distance phone call for you. It's from Chicago."

Bobby left the table. He hurried to the phone. On the other end of the line was Mr. Wilson—the scout who had discovered Bobby seven years before.

"Hello."

"Hello, Bobby. How are you? This is Mr. Wilson."

"Fine," said Bobby.

"I'd like you to play tonight," said Mr. Wilson.

"The Black Hawks will be in town. They'll be playing an exhibition game against the Rangers. Can you make it?"

"Yes Sir, I'll be ready."

That night Bobby was ready. He played an outstanding game. He scored two goals against the Rangers.

Late in the night, after the game, Mr. and Mrs. Hull were asked to come to St. Catherine's. Bobby was excited. Mr. Wilson asked the Hulls if Bobby could become a pro. They said yes. Bobby, at 18, became one of the youngest National Hockey League players. It was 1957.

The Hawks needed Bobby. In the last four years they had come in last in the National Hockey League. They had not won the Stanley Cup, the prize that goes

to the best team in the League, since 1938. The stands in the Chicago Stadium were seldom filled.

Bobby didn't become the Golden Jet in his first year of pro hockey. He wasn't used to the new kind of action. Older defensemen pushed him around. Thousands of fans were in the stands, yelling and screaming. The pros played rough hockey.

Bobby played seven games before he even scored his first goal. It wasn't a flashy goal. Bobby got knocked down and fell on the ice. He then slid into the net on top of the puck. He had yet to show his greatness.

In the first year Bobby scored 13 goals. Fans recognized his blond hair. He was fast and strong. In his second year of play, 1958-1959, he scored 18 goals. Goalies began to fear him.

During the 1959-1960 season Bobby was 21 years old. That year he won the scoring title with 39 goals and 42 assists. As the fastest skater in the League he could travel 28 miles per hour on the ice. He shot across the ice like a jet. He had thick legs that helped him speed away from dead stops.

Bobby's biceps (upper arm muscles) were 17½ inches in circumference. They were bigger than Muhammad Ali's! When defensemen surrounded him he pushed them aside with his strong arms. He could break through two men and still control the puck. His arm was like a slingshot. Many checking defensemen would bounce off him. A player from another team said, "Checking Hull is like crashing into cement." He could hold a man away with one hand and score a goal with his free hand. He was 5 feet 10 inches tall. Bobby weighed 195 pounds.

Bobby's most fearsome shot was the slap shot. Many fans believe Bobby was the one who made it popular. He would be as much as 70 feet away from the net before he would shoot. He would wind up. He would bring his stick high above his head, then swing it down. Wham! The puck would zoom through the air. It traveled at 118 miles per hour. It landed in the net. The red light lit up. Another goal!

Pucks he hit could knock goalies down into their nets. His shots would hit so hard against goalies' leg pads that they would leave marks on the goalies' legs. Once Bobby hit a puck for a low drive and it hit a Toronto player's steel tipped skate-boot. A toe inside broke! Even before a goalie could dive at Bobby's puck, the puck would be flying into the net.

Fans would watch for his blond head of hair. When they saw it rocket across the ice, they stood up and screamed, "Go, Bobby, go!" He charged towards the net. The Golden Jet was on the move again.

It was around Christmas time in Chicago. One day Bobby went to the arena to practice. When he looked towards the ice he saw a pretty red-headed girl skating. Her name was Joanne McKay. She was a figure-skater who worked in an ice show. Bobby liked her right away. Later they were married. She was his second wife. They get along well. Joanne knows how to keep Bobby calm on the day of a game. She knows he can't sit still. She tells how they went on a vacation once and after two days of sitting in the sun, he told her, "I can't take it any longer! Let's go home." He sometimes comes home after a game like a growling bear. Joanne says, "You tell 'em, Star."

Since Bobby had joined the Hawks in 1957 the team had improved. In his first year the Hawks took fifth place. In his second year with the team, they won third place. The next two years Chicago made second place.

The next season, 1960-1961, Chicago hockey fans went wild! The Black Hawks had not won the Stanley Cup in 23 years. They sensed that this might be the year.

After beating Montreal in six tough games, they faced the Detroit Red Wings. In the first game Hull scored two goals as Chicago won 3-2. Detroit came back and won the next one 3-1. Two of the greatest hockey players of all time were on the ice, Gordie Howe and Bobby Hull. The next two games were split, each team won one of them. Chicago won the fifth game 6-3. In that game, Bobby's teammate, Stan Mikita scored 2 goals.

The Hawks were now hungry for the Cup. A few nights later it snowed in Detroit. The same night the Hawks won 5-1. The Cup was theirs!

In 1963 the Hawks were again playing the Detroit Red Wings for the Stanley Cup. It was a tough battle! In the first game Bobby scored two goals. In the second game Bobby was rushing towards the net with the puck. Suddenly Bruce MacGregor's stick hit Bobby in the nose. A loud smack filled the air! Bobby fell to the ice. He was almost knocked out. His teammates helped him to the locker room. Blood was everywhere. Bobby's nose was badly broken.

The next game the Hawks played without Bobby and lost. Five days after breaking his nose, Bobby was on the ice again. It was the third game. His eyes were black and his nose was puffed up. Bobby scored a goal but the Hawks lost. During the game Bobby got hit in the nose again. The doctor had to reset the broken bone.

Bobby scored another goal in the next game. But it was no use. Detroit won the game.

It was the sixth game of the series. Detroit was ahead 3 games to 2 games. Chicago was in trouble. Both teams wanted that Cup. The lead changed hands—back and forth. Bobby scored, then Detroit. Finally, Detroit won the game 7-4.

By the end of the game Bobby had scored 3

goals and had one assist. His face hurt all over. His
eyes were watery. He had been under very heavy
pressure. Fans agreed that his bravery while playing
was one of the greatest moments in hockey.

During the 1961-1962 season, Bobby was in his
fifth year in the League. Many hockey fans thought
he could score 50 goals. He had yet to do it. Only
two hockey players, Maurice "the Rocket" Richard and
Bernie "Boom Boom" Geoffrian had scored 50 goals
in one season. As the season came to an end, Bobby
scored goal number 50. He had tied a record.

Year after year Bobby made the All-Star team.
He helped Chicago make the play-offs every year. Bobby
is so fast that it is hard to stop him and still follow
the rules. Many players try to stop him by tripping,

hooking, or fouling him. But peaceful Bobby hardly ever fights back. His peaceful nature helped him win one of hockey's highest awards in 1964—the Lady Byng Trophy. The trophy stood for good sportsmanship. That same year he won the Most Valuable Player Award. Only one other player has won both awards in one year. The Coach said, "Bobby's almost too good to be true." Someone from another team said, "On or off the ice, Hull is a great advertisement for hockey."

He is the world's fastest player in the world's fastest game. Speed, power—across the ice—44 feet per second—the puck at the end of his stick, when you watch Bobby Hull you see what hockey is all about. Thousands of fans watch him play. He was the king of hockey. To Mr. Hockey it seemed simple. He played hockey because he really enjoyed it. U. S. 1962240

As Bobby scored goal after goal, defensemen tried to stop him. They checked him all the time. Many defensemen had only one job. Stop Bobby Hull! They tripped him and held onto his arms. Two or three defensemen surrounded him when he had the puck. He became the most feared player in hockey. He complained, "You turn away from one man and there's another on you."

Over the years the rough play was hard on Bobby. His nose, which has been broken more than once, sticks to one side. He has had cuts all over his

face. He has had more than 200 stitches taken. All his front teeth are gone. He even played with a broken jaw. Coach Reay says, "As long as Bobby can stand up he wants to be out there on the ice."

Bobby knows how dangerous hockey is and his attitude seems to be that he doesn't ever want to seriously hurt anyone, but goalies really take their chances. It's one thing to get hit by a flying puck or by accident, but another to get hit with a stick or a fist.

Even easy-going Bobby blows up once in awhile. A Detroit Red Wing was giving him a hard time and Bobby hit back. Bobby's stick to the player's head caused a cut that needed 18 stitches. Bobby was sorry later, and he said that wasn't the way he liked to play the game but he had to protect himself.

On March 12, 1966, over 20,000 fans filled the Chicago Stadium. The Hawks were playing the New York Rangers. All season defensemen had tried to stop Hull. In spite of it all he had 50 goals. Could he break the record and score another goal? No hockey player in history had scored more than 50 goals. Since scoring his 50th goal, four games had passed. It was the third period. The Rangers were ahead 2-1.

A pass came to Hull. He looked ahead toward the net. Cesare Maniago, the goalie, was getting ready. Bobby skated between two defensemen. He was 40 feet from the net. He raised his stick. Wham! The puck

flew under the goalie's right leg. The red light went on. Bobby had scored his 51st goal.

The fans went wild! They screamed and stomped their feet. Hats were thrown onto the ice. Bobby picked up one of the hats and put it on his head. He had a big smile on his face. The fans cheered for 10 minutes. They had seen one of the greatest goals in hockey history.

Bobby had played for the National Hockey League for 15 years. He had been signed up with the Black Hawks for 22 years. With the Hawks he was making $150,000 a year. He made more money by letting companies put his name on hockey sticks and pucks they made. A boy can also buy a Bobby Hull T-shirt. Bobby Hull has helped sell clothes, cars and tractors. Adding everything up, Bobby was making very good money.

In 1972, a new hockey league was formed. It was called the World Hockey Association. The League formed teams in Chicago, Boston, Ottawa, and other cities. The League was shaky. Many men could lose thousands of dollars if the League didn't make it. The owners had to do something to get the League off to a good start. They needed a star to join their league, then the other hockey players would follow. The owners asked the biggest star of all — Bobby Hull.

Each team in the new league put money into a fund. The sum came to $1,000,000. They offered this money to Bobby Hull. He thought about it for a long time. Should he leave his old team the Black Hawks? Or should he try on a new team?

It was July of 1972. After much thinking, Bobby decided to join the new league. He received a check for $1,000,000. Then he signed with the Winnipeg Jets for $250,000 a year. He was to become a player-coach. Within a few minutes he became a rich man—a millionaire.

Bobby looks forward to playing with the Winnipeg Jets. He feels that many people are looking to them as their leader.

More than anything Bobby Hull is a great hockey player. In the town of Pointe Anne hangs a sign, "Pointe Anne, Birthplace of Bobby Hull, World's Greatest Hockey Player." Fans jump up out of their seats when he is on a breakaway. They scream when he raises his stick and makes a slap shot. And yell, "Go, Bobby, Go," when he zooms toward the net with the puck. After a game they crowd around, trying to touch or talk to him.

The "Golden Jet" became such a hero because of who he was as well as because of how well he played. Even fans from other teams cheered Bobby. They seemed to feel that if their team lost, at least it was superstar Hull who had beaten them.

Bobby is a warm man. When he played in Chicago, he visited children in hospitals. He always has time to sign autographs. Other players respected his fairness and sportsmanship. When reporters talk with him, he is full of life and good will.

As soon as the season is over, Bobby heads for his farm in Ontario. He doesn't like big cities. He calls himself a small town guy. He likes the people who live around him and feels close to them.

On the farm, Bobby raises cattle. He likes to chop wood and stack hay. He wants his three sons, Bob, Blake, and Brett to grow up in the country. As much as he loves hockey, he dreams of the time when his days of traveling from one city to another will be over. He longs to be a full-time farmer.

Bobby's life began over 30 years ago. Then, he was the boy who loved to put on skates and walk to the lake. It was early in the morning. The sun was just coming up. He skated all day with a stick in his hands. The cold didn't bother him. When the sun set, and darkness came, he was on the ice. He's still on the ice—the Golden Jet—the World's Greatest Hockey Player!

JACK NICKLAUS
BILL RUSSELL
MARK SPITZ
VINCE LOMBARDI
BILLIE JEAN KING
ROBERTO CLEMENTE
JOE NAMATH
BOBBY HULL
HANK AARON
JERRY WEST
TOM SEAVER
JACKIE ROBINSON
MUHAMMAD ALI
O. J. SIMPSON
JOHNNY BENCH
WILT CHAMBERLAIN
ARNOLD PALMER
A. J. FOYT
JOHNNY UNITAS
GORDIE HOWE

# superstars!
# superstars!
# superstars

CREATIVE EDUCATION SPORTS SUPERSTARS

WALT FRAZIER
PHIL AND TONY ESPOSITO
BOB GRIESE
FRANK ROBINSON
PANCHO GONZALES
LEE TREVINO
KAREEM ABDUL JABBAR
JEAN CLAUDE KILLY
EVONNE GOOLAGONG
ARTHUR ASHE
SECRETARIAT
ROGER STAUBACK
FRAN TARKENTON
BOBBY ORR
LARRY CSONKA
BILL WALTON
ALAN PAGE
PEGGY FLEMING
OLGA KORBUT
DON SCHULA
MICKEY MANTLE